THE SCIENCE OF
FORCES

PROJECTS AND EXPERIMENTS WITH FORCES AND MACHINES

TABLETOP SCIENTIST

STEVE PARKER

Heinemann
LIBRARY

CONTENTS

From the force which keeps us on Earth, called gravity…

…to whirring motors and sparks caused by friction…

…to the complex and delicate gears in a clock, forces are at work around us all the time.

INTRODUCTION

Machines, mechanical devices, and gadgets are always at hand. We use them every day – from a simple door handle or can-opener, to more complex types like disc players and cars. All of these machines need forces to make them go. Forces push, pull, press, lift, squeeze, stretch, bend or turn. When we pedal a bicycle, we make a force. In other cases, motors and engines make the forces for us, like a truck's diesel engine or the motor in an electric toothbrush. The science of forces, motion, and machines is known as mechanics. It allows engineers and inventors to devise new gadgets and devices that make our lives easier.

HOW IT WORKS

These panels explain the scientific ideas on which each project is based, and the processes that make it work.

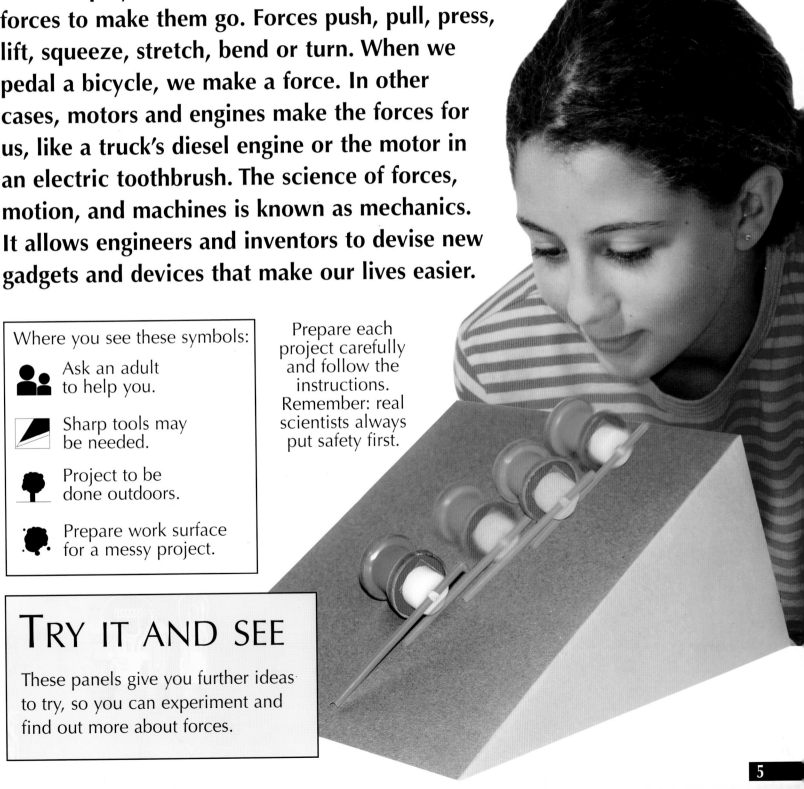

Where you see these symbols:

Ask an adult to help you.

Sharp tools may be needed.

Project to be done outdoors.

Prepare work surface for a messy project.

Prepare each project carefully and follow the instructions. Remember: real scientists always put safety first.

TRY IT AND SEE

These panels give you further ideas to try, so you can experiment and find out more about forces.

5

FORCE ALL AROUND

One force acts on you and everything else, all the time, everywhere you go – unless you're in deep space. This is the force of gravity. Any object has the pulling force of gravity. The amount of gravity depends on the object's mass. The Earth is huge, so its gravity is strong. It pulls objects down, giving them what we call 'weight'.

Our planet's gravity extends 400,000 km to the Moon and keeps it pulled near to the Earth.

PROJECT: MAKE A WEIGHING MACHINE

WEIGHING MACHINE

WHAT YOU NEED

- **large and small cardboard boxes**
- **dowel**
- **thick card**
- **thick marker pen**
- **thin and thick wire**
- **split-pin paper fastener**
- **plastic cup**
- **weights**
- **scissors**

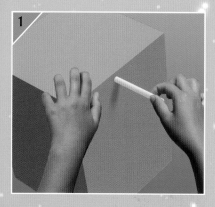

1 PUSH THE DOWEL THROUGH THE LARGER BOX, FROM ONE SIDE TO THE OTHER, NEAR THE TOP.

2 CURL THICK WIRE ROUND A MARKER PEN TO MAKE A SPRING. HANG IT ON THE DOWEL.

3 MAKE TWO SLITS IN A PLASTIC CUP. SLIDE THROUGH A NARROW PIECE OF CARD FOR THE POINTER.

4 CUT A LONG SLOT IN ONE SIDE OF THE SMALLER BOX, NEAR THE UPPER CORNER.

5 PUSH THE PAPER-FASTENER THROUGH THE END OF THE POINTER AND INTO THE SLOT.

6 GLUE THE SMALLER BOX TO THE LARGE ONE. HANG THE CUP ON THE SPRING WITH THIN WIRE.

MASS & WEIGHT

All objects have mass. However, objects only have weight when the force of gravity acts on them. The Earth's gravity pulls things which have mass towards the centre of the planet. Gravity keeps us 'stuck' to the surface of the Earth! Far away in space there is no gravity, and so no weight either.

SPRING STRETCHED

FORCE OF GRAVITY PULLS OBJECT DOWNWARDS

MORE MASS = LONGER SPRING

ADJUST THE SPRING SO THE POINTER IS AT THE TOP OF THE SLOT WHEN THE CUP IS EMPTY. PUT AN ITEM SUCH AS A BALL-BEARING OR PEBBLE INTO THE CUP. THE FORCE OF EARTH'S GRAVITY PULLS IT DOWN AND STRETCHES THE SPRING. THE POINTER SHOWS THE ITEM'S WEIGHT — THE AMOUNT OF GRAVITATIONAL PULL ON IT. ADD MORE ITEMS TO THE CUP. THEIR EXTRA MASS MEANS A GREATER PULL OF GRAVITY, MAKING THE SPRING LONGER.

EQUAL STRETCH

If you have lots of identical items, like toy building blocks or ball-bearings, try adding them to the cup one at a time. Mark the position of the pointer each time with a pen. Are the gaps between the marks equal?

EQUALLY-SPACED MARKS MEAN THE SPRING STRETCHES BY THE SAME AMOUNT FOR THE SAME ADDED MASS. (THIS FOLLOWS A SCIENTIFIC RULE CALLED HOOKE'S LAW.) UNTIL THE LOAD BECOMES TOO HEAVY...

STOP-GO FORCES

A football does not move until you kick it. Any object which is not moving will stay still, unless a force acts on it to make it go. Once the object is moving, it will keep going unless a force makes it slow down and stop. These forces are normally fairly obvious, such as brakes in a car.

As a skydiver falls faster, air pushes back with increasing force until a steady speed is reached.

In 1997 the force of Thrust SSC's jet engines was enough to make this car the world's speediest. It went faster than sound: 1,225 km/h.

PROJECT: BUILD A CATAPULT

CATAPULT

WHAT YOU NEED

- **stiff card**
- **straw**
- **elastic band**
- **small box**
- **small test objects**
- **glue**
- **scissors**

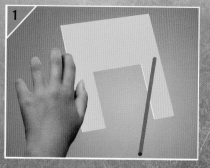

1 CUT A U-SHAPED FRAME OF STIFF CARD, ABOUT THE SAME HEIGHT AS THE DRINKING STRAW.

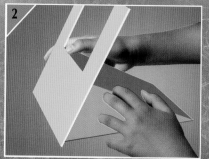

2 CUT THE CORNER FROM A CARDBOARD BOX TO MAKE A TRIANGULAR BASE FOR THE U.

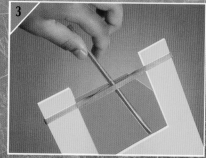

3 STRETCH AN ELASTIC BAND OVER THE U. PUT A STRAW THROUGH IT AND WIND IT AROUND.

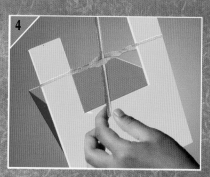

4 POSITION THE STRAW SO ITS LOWER END RESTS ON THE FRONT OF THE FRAME'S BASE.

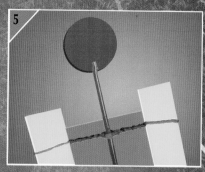

5 SLIT THE STRAW'S UPPER END. GLUE A ROUND PIECE OF CARD INTO IT FOR THE LAUNCH PAD.

FAST TO SLOW

The band provides the firing force to launch the item. Why doesn't it keep going? Because of two other forces. Gravity pulls the item down. And as the item pushes aside air, the air pushes back with a force called air resistance, which slows it down.

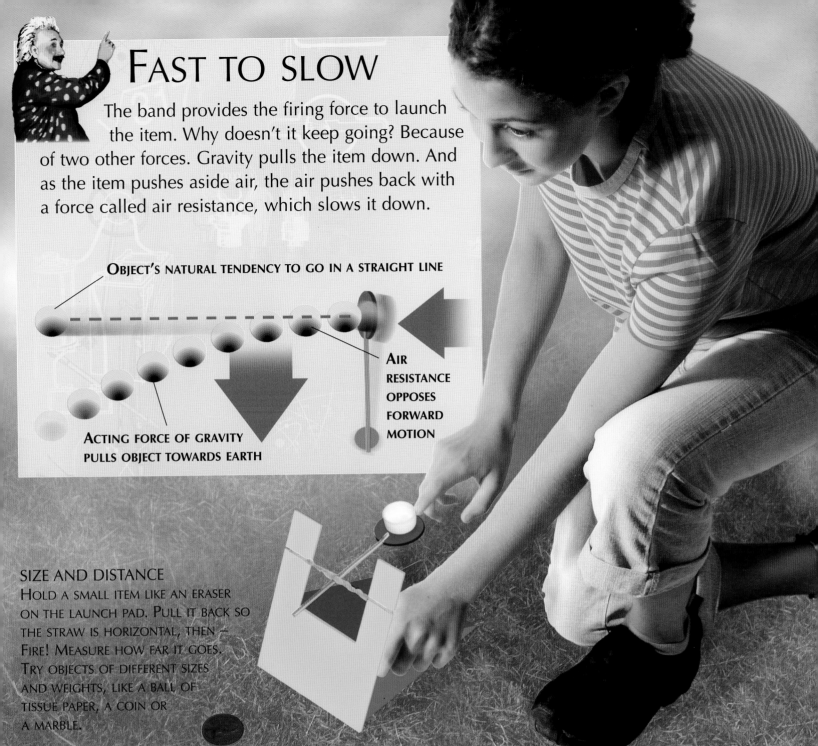

OBJECT'S NATURAL TENDENCY TO GO IN A STRAIGHT LINE

AIR RESISTANCE OPPOSES FORWARD MOTION

ACTING FORCE OF GRAVITY PULLS OBJECT TOWARDS EARTH

SIZE AND DISTANCE

HOLD A SMALL ITEM LIKE AN ERASER ON THE LAUNCH PAD. PULL IT BACK SO THE STRAW IS HORIZONTAL, THEN — FIRE! MEASURE HOW FAR IT GOES. TRY OBJECTS OF DIFFERENT SIZES AND WEIGHTS, LIKE A BALL OF TISSUE PAPER, A COIN OR A MARBLE.

MORE OR LESS

Try different amounts of firing force. For the same item, pull the launch pad back only a little way, then next time, as far as possible.

WEIGH DIFFERENT ITEMS AS SHOWN ON PAGE 7. ARE HEAVIER ONES FIRED FARTHER?

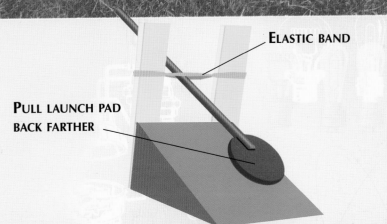

ELASTIC BAND

PULL LAUNCH PAD BACK FARTHER

GETTING GOING

Forces can make things move. If something is still, it needs a force to get it going. The more mass an object has, the more force is needed to do this. Also, the longer a force is applied, the faster the object moves.

A huge, heavy freight train has a large mass. It may take half an hour for the locomotive's tremendous pulling force to bring it up to a steady speed.

PROJECT: MAKE A FORCE-METER

FORCE-METER

WHAT YOU NEED

- **stiff card**
- **thick polyboard**
- **two beads**
- **elastic band**
- **strong thread**
- **eyelet**
- **drawing pin**
- **glue**
- **scissors**

CUT A RECTANGLE OF STIFF CARD AND TWO SLIGHTLY SHORTER, MUCH NARROWER PIECES OF THICK POLYBOARD.

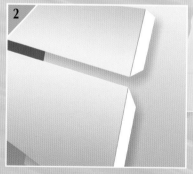

TRIM A LONG EDGE OF EACH POLYBOARD AT AN ANGLE, SO THEY FORM A V-SHAPED TUNNEL WHEN PUT TOGETHER.

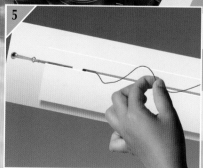

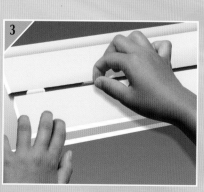

GLUE THE POLYBOARD PIECES TO THE CARD, SO THE BEADS CAN SLIDE ALONG FREELY INSIDE THE TUNNEL FROM END TO END.

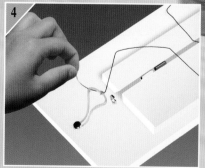

FIX AN ELASTIC BAND TO THE CARD'S END WITH A DRAWING PIN. TIE IT TO THE THREAD.

PASS THE THREAD THROUGH AN EYELET FIXED IN FRONT OF THE TUNNEL, KNOT IT, AND PASS IT THROUGH THE TWO BEADS.

FORCES MOVE MASS

Anything that moves has kinetic energy. If an object is still, a force must give it enough kinetic energy to move. Objects with a bigger mass have more kinetic energy when moving, so they need a larger force to get started. Vary the weight of the load in the truck and compare the readings on the force-meter.

INCREASED LOAD

FORCE NEEDED TO MAKE TRUCK MOVE

HEAVE AWAY!
GLUE ON A PAPER SCALE OF LINES. TIE A WHEELED TOY SUCH AS A TRUCK TO THE STRING. GRADUALLY PULL IT HARDER WITH THE FORCE-METER. NOTE THE SCALE READING JUST AS IT STARTS TO MOVE.

MORE MASS = MORE FORCE

Try loading a toy truck with identical weights, such as building bricks or ball bearings. As the load gets bigger in equal amounts, brick by brick, do the readings on the scale go up by equal amounts too?

SPEED UP, SLOW DOWN

A plane can cruise at one speed for hours. But for take-off it has to go faster and faster on the runway. On landing it has to lose speed. Great forces are needed to do this. Speeding up is acceleration. Slowing down is deceleration.

A dragster accelerates at 40 metres per second per second. After reaching a top speed of 500 km/h, it needs a parachute to slow it down.

PROJECT: BUILD AN INK-DRIP ACCELEROMETER

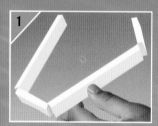

1 MAKE A CART FRAME OF THICK CARD, TO FIT AROUND THE TWO COTTON REELS.

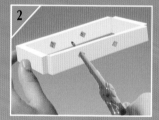

2 MAKE TWO HOLES IN THE SIDES OF THE CART, FOR EACH STRAW AXLE.

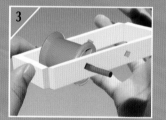

3 PUSH THE STRAWS THROUGH THE HOLES AND COTTON REELS.

4 PUSH A SMALL BLOB OF MODELLING CLAY INTO THE FUNNEL'S NARROW TIP. PIERCE WITH A PIN.

5 ADJUST THE PIERCED HOLE'S SIZE SO THAT INK IN THE FUNNEL EMERGES WITH REGULAR DRIPS.

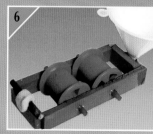

6 FIX THE EMPTY FUNNEL TO THE CART'S BACK. USE MODELLING CLAY TO BALANCE THE CART.

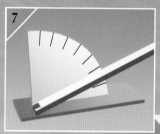

7 CUT A LONG RAMP OF CARD. TAPE IT TO THE CARD BASE. ADD A QUARTER-CIRCLE SCALE.

FASTER, FASTER

The force of gravity pulls the cart down the ramp. As the cart accelerates, gravity continues to pull, so the cart gains yet more speed. The drips come out of the funnel at regular time intervals. If the ramp is at a steep angle, the cart accelerates more rapidly, and travels farther between each drip.

DRIP MARKS AT INCREASING INTERVALS SHOW ACCELERATION

EVEN GREATER SPACING MEANS HIGHER ACCELERATION

DRIP-DRIP FLYER
PUT A LONG STRIP OF BLOTTING PAPER ON THE RAMP FOR EACH RUN. ADD SOME INK TO THE FUNNEL, LIFT THE RAMP, AND LET THE CART GO. MAKE SURE THE CART AIMS STRAIGHT DOWN THE RAMP!

DOES MASS MATTER?

Changing the ramp's angle affects the rate of acceleration. What about changing the cart's mass? For the same angle, compare drips for the basic cart and with extra weight.

WEIGHT

ACT AND REACT

White-hot gases forced downwards from the rear of a rocket are its action. The reaction is to push the rocket upwards – all the way into space.

When you push a wall, you exert a force on it. Why doesn't the wall fall over? It pushes back with a force equal to your own, but in the opposite direction. Your force is the action. The wall's is the reaction. This is part of a scientific law: 'For every action there is an equal and opposite reaction.'

Swimmers push the water powerfully backwards. The reaction is that their bodies are pushed forwards.

PROJECT: BUILD AN ACTION/REACTION RAMP

ACTION/ REACTION RAMP

WHAT YOU NEED

- stiff card
- marbles
- string
- pencil
- glue
- scissors

1. MARK A SHALLOW CURVE ON CARD USING STRING WITH A PENCIL AT ONE END AND THE OTHER END FIXED.

2. CUT OUT THE SHAPE. PLACE IT ON CARD, MARK AROUND IT, AND CUT OUT A SECOND IDENTICAL SHAPE.

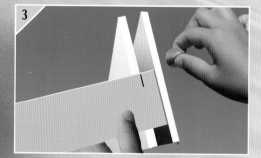

3. CUT SEVERAL NARROW STRIPS OF CARD, ALL THE SAME WIDTH – SLIGHTLY NARROWER THAN A MARBLE.

4. GLUE THE SHAPES TOGETHER WITH THE NARROW LENGTHS OF CARD BETWEEN, FORMING A U-SHAPE.

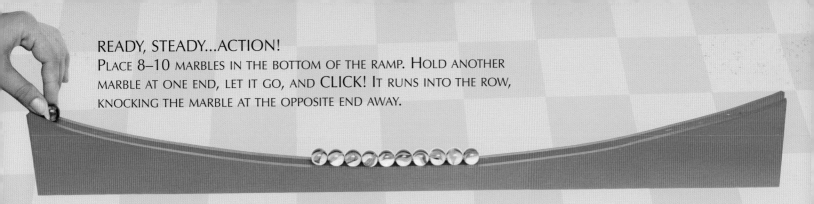

EQUAL HITS - ONE IN, ONE OUT

As the force of gravity pulls the marble down the slope, it gains more and more kinetic energy. When it hits the row of marbles, they push back with the same force in the opposite direction. The first marble stops, but its energy passes to the second marble, then third, and so on along the row. The last marble is free to move and rolls away. Then...

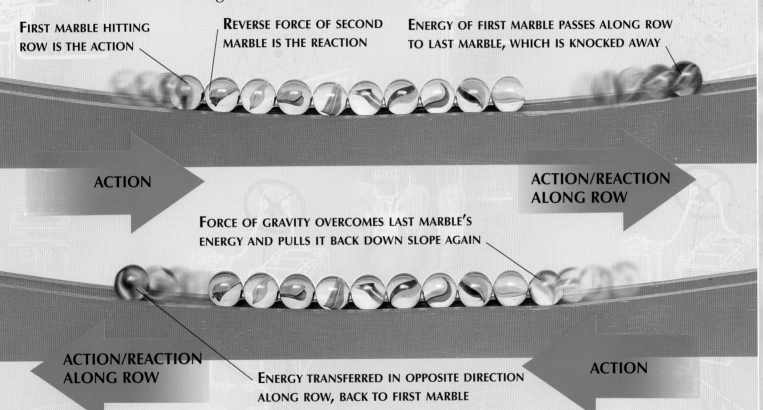

FIRST MARBLE HITTING ROW IS THE ACTION

REVERSE FORCE OF SECOND MARBLE IS THE REACTION

ENERGY OF FIRST MARBLE PASSES ALONG ROW TO LAST MARBLE, WHICH IS KNOCKED AWAY

ACTION

ACTION/REACTION ALONG ROW

FORCE OF GRAVITY OVERCOMES LAST MARBLE'S ENERGY AND PULLS IT BACK DOWN SLOPE AGAIN

ACTION/REACTION ALONG ROW

ENERGY TRANSFERRED IN OPPOSITE DIRECTION ALONG ROW, BACK TO FIRST MARBLE

ACTION

MORE MARBLES

Try increasing the force by releasing two marbles to roll into the ramp. Are two marbles knocked away from the other end? What about three, four or more? Why do the to-and-fro movements gradually slow and stop? (Page 18 may give you one clue.)

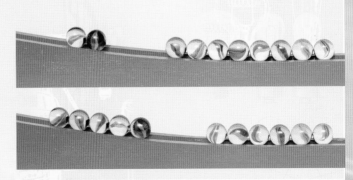

LOADS OF EFFORT

A lever can use a fairly small force at one end to produce a very large force at the other – enough to lift the lid off a paint can.

Can you lift a truck? Perhaps, if you had a lever long enough. A lever is a simple machine that alters a force. It is a stiff rod that tilts, or pivots, from a place called the fulcrum. A lever can make a small force into a huge one. Levers range from the tiniest nail clippers to giant cranes.

The effort is the force needed to move a lever. A crane's tilting jib is like a lever with the fulcrum at one end, the effort near the other, and the load on the cable.

PROJECT: BUILD AN ADJUSTABLE LEVER

ADJUSTABLE LEVER

WHAT YOU NEED

- larger and smaller card tubes (such as mailing tubes)
- card sheet
- cardboard box
- string
- weights
- glue
- scissors

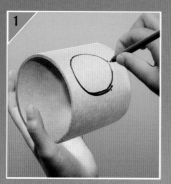

CUT A SHORT LENGTH FROM A WIDE CARD TUBE. DRAW AROUND A SMALLER TUBE ON EACH SIDE OF THE LARGER ONE.

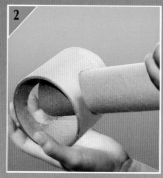

CUT AROUND THESE LINES TO MAKE TWO HOLES IN THE LARGER TUBE. PUSH THE SMALLER LEVER TUBE THROUGH THEM.

CUT A SLIGHTLY LONGER PIECE OF THE LARGER TUBE. THEN CUT THIS IN HALF TO MAKE A GUTTER-SHAPED CRADLE.

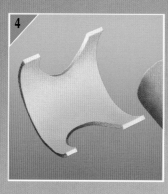

CUT A U SHAPED NOTCH IN EACH SIDE OF THE CRADLE, WIDE ENOUGH FOR THE SMALLER TUBE.

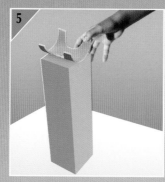

GLUE THE CRADLE TO THE TOP OF A TALL BOX. GLUE THE BOX TO A WIDE CARD BASE TO MAKE IT STABLE.

REST THE LEVER IN THE CRADLE OR FULCRUM. PREPARE LOOPED STRINGS FOR EFFORT AND LOAD.

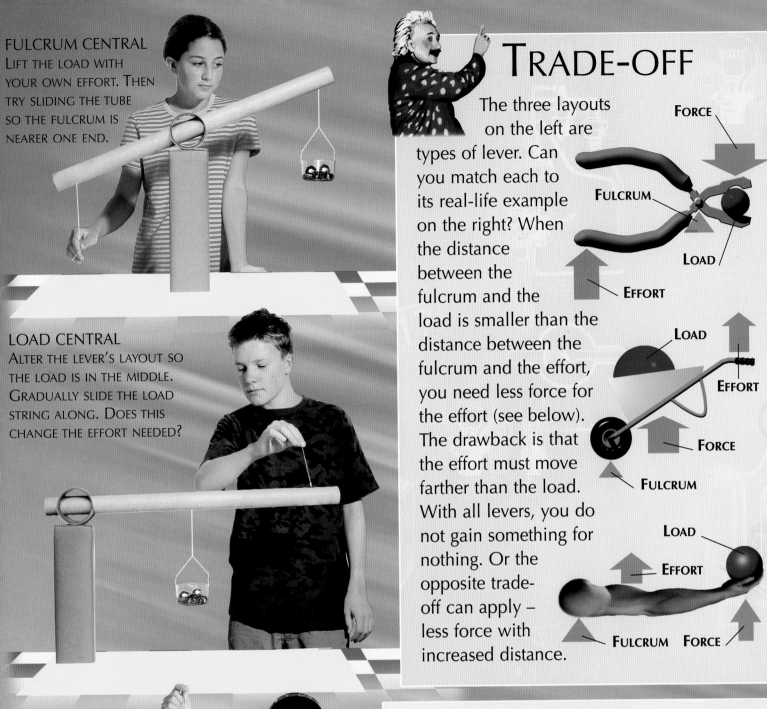

FULCRUM CENTRAL

LIFT THE LOAD WITH YOUR OWN EFFORT. THEN TRY SLIDING THE TUBE SO THE FULCRUM IS NEARER ONE END.

TRADE-OFF

The three layouts on the left are types of lever. Can you match each to its real-life example on the right? When the distance between the fulcrum and the load is smaller than the distance between the fulcrum and the effort, you need less force for the effort (see below). The drawback is that the effort must move farther than the load. With all levers, you do not gain something for nothing. Or the opposite trade-off can apply – less force with increased distance.

FORCE
FULCRUM
LOAD
EFFORT

LOAD
EFFORT
FORCE
FULCRUM

LOAD
EFFORT
FULCRUM   FORCE

LOAD CENTRAL

ALTER THE LEVER'S LAYOUT SO THE LOAD IS IN THE MIDDLE. GRADUALLY SLIDE THE LOAD STRING ALONG. DOES THIS CHANGE THE EFFORT NEEDED?

EFFORT CENTRAL

WITH THIS LAYOUT, TRY MOVING THE EFFORT NEARER THE FULCRUM, THEN NEARER THE LOAD.

BIGGER BUT SMALLER

As the position of the fulcrum changes, the force of the effort needed to move the same load also alters. Try measuring this changing effort with the weighing machine from page 7.

LONG DISTANCE TO EFFORT

SHORT DISTANCE TO EFFORT

FORCE AND FRICTION

Friction from a grinding disc is used to shape the hardest metal or rock.

You need more force to drag a rough rock across stony ground, than to slide a smooth rock over slippery ice. As uneven surfaces rub and scrape against each other they oppose the force moving them. This is known as friction.

Ball-bearings are made of very hard, smooth metal. They have almost no friction and so move smoothly.

PROJECT: THE CLIMBING CRAWLER

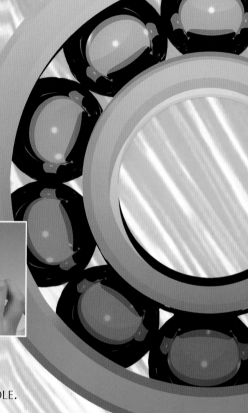

CLIMBING CRAWLER

1

CUT A SHORT PIECE OF CANDLE. MAKE A HOLE THROUGH THE MIDDLE WITH A NAIL.

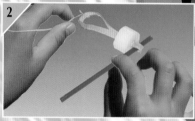

2

LOOP AN ELASTIC BAND OVER A SHORT STRAW AND THROUGH THE CANDLE'S HOLE.

WHAT YOU NEED

- wax candle
- drinking straw
- elastic bands
- cotton reel
- smooth plastic
- staple or paper clip
- card slope
- materials to put on slope
- nail

3

PUT THE REST OF THE ELASTIC BAND THROUGH A COTTON REEL.

4

FIX THE BAND'S END TO THE REEL WITH A STAPLE OR PAPER CLIP.

5

WIND UP THE ELASTIC BAND, USING THE STRAW AS A HANDLE.

5

TEST THE CRAWLER ON A SLOPE. NOTE HOW WELL IT CLIMBS.

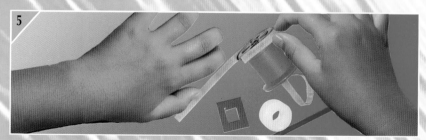

5

TRY SOME CHANGES. PUT SHORT ELASTIC BANDS AROUND THE REEL'S RIMS AND A PLASTIC 'WASHER' BETWEEN THE CANDLE AND THE REEL.

GRIP AND SLIP

Rough surfaces increase friction. Smooth ones reduce it. There is less friction acting on the straw's turning force where the candle rubs on the cotton reel, and more friction where the reel's rims rub on the slope.

WAX CANDLE SLIPS OVER PLASTIC WASHER

ELASTIC-BAND RIM GRIPS PAPER SLOPE

FASTER CRAWLER
DOES THE 'NEW IMPROVED' CRAWLER CLIMB THE SLOPE FASTER? DO ALL THE TESTS CAREFULLY, WINDING THE BAND THE SAME AMOUNT EACH TIME.

GRIPPIER, SLIPPIER

Try further improvements. Add a few drops of cooking oil lubricant between the candle and the plastic washer. Does this make the crawler climb better? Make the slope of rougher material, like sandpaper, then time the new crawler again.

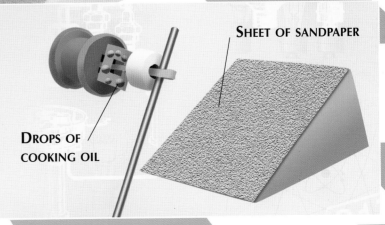

SHEET OF SANDPAPER

DROPS OF COOKING OIL

ROUND AND ROUND

It takes a huge force to stop an oil-tanker going at top speed. Moving objects tend to keep moving – this is momentum. The bigger an object, and the faster it moves, the greater its momentum. This can be in a straight line or in a curve or circle, called angular momentum.

An ultra-fast spinning gyroscope has **massive angular momentum, which makes it resist tilting.**

Without the inward pull of the chains, the people on a merry-go-round ride would fly off.

PROJECT: MAKE SOME SPINNING TOPS

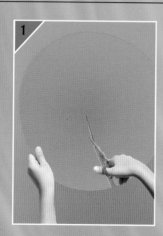

1

CUT OUT A DINNER-PLATE-SIZED CIRCLE OF STIFF CARD. MAKE A STRAIGHT SLIT FROM EDGE TO CENTRE.

2

PULL THE EDGES OVER EACH OTHER AND TAPE THEM TO FORM A WIDE CONE ARENA. REST THIS IN A BASE, LIKE A BOWL.

3

CUT OUT SOME 10 CM DISCS OF STIFF CARD. DECORATE THEM WITH VARIOUS COLOURS AND PATTERNS.

4

PUSH A SHORT, BLUNT PENCIL THROUGH EACH DISC'S CENTRE, SO THAT ABOUT 2 CM PENCIL LENGTH IS BENEATH.

FORCED TO SPIN

When you twirl the top, you apply a force to give it angular momentum. As the top turns, its shape means that a force, known as centripetal force, pulls the card of the disc inwards all the time. The tiny bits of card making up the disc try to carry on in straight lines, according to the law of motion. But the strength of the card prevents this happening.

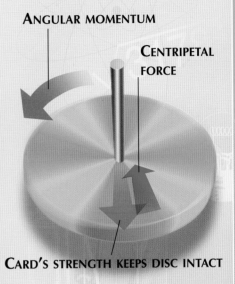

ANGULAR MOMENTUM

CENTRIPETAL FORCE

CARD'S STRENGTH KEEPS DISC INTACT

MORE = MORE?

A top's momentum depends on its mass and its speed. Make a top heavier with modelling clay. It needs a bigger force to start but does it spin for longer?

TRY ADDING THE CLAY AS A LUMP AROUND THE CENTRE OR AS A RING AROUND THE DISC'S RIM.

MODELLING CLAY

TWIRLING TOPS AT TOP SPEED

PUT A TOP IN THE CONE ARENA, HOLDING IT BY THE UPPER END OF THE PENCIL. FLICK YOUR FINGERS TO MAKE IT TWIRL AROUND. PRACTISE THIS MOVEMENT SO THE TOP GAINS SPINNING SPEED OVER A SECOND OR SO, RATHER THAN TRYING TO TWIRL IT FAST IMMEDIATELY. THE TOP TURNS...AND TURNS...STAYING UPRIGHT FOR SOME TIME. AS IT SLOWS, IT STARTS TO WOBBLE. FINALLY IT TIPS ON TO ITS EDGE AND STOPS. HOW LONG CAN YOU KEEP A TOP SPINNING?

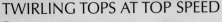

PULLING POWER

A pulley is a wheel with raised rims, so that a rope, cable or chain fits around it. One pulley can change the direction of a force, so that if you pull a rope downwards, the load moves upwards. Two pulleys make it easier to raise the load.

Sets of pulleys are common on cranes, hoists, elevators, and sailing ships. They allow a small pulling force to move a large load – even a huge, heavy sail filled with wind.

PROJECT: BUILD A TWO-PULLEY HOIST

TWO-PULLEY HOIST

WHAT YOU NEED

- thick card
- cardboard tube or dowel
- polyboard or polystyrene
- string
- glue
- scissors

CUT OUT FOUR LARGE CIRCLES, ALL OF THE SAME SIZE, FROM THICK CARD.

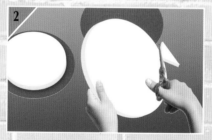

CUT TWO SLIGHTLY SMALLER CIRCLES FROM THICK POLYBOARD OR POLYSTYRENE SHEET.

SANDWICH EACH SMALLER CIRCLE BETWEEN TWO LARGER ONES. GLUE TO MAKE A PULLEY.

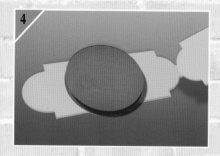

CUT SIDES FOR THE UPPER FRAME FROM THICK CARD AS SHOWN, USING ONE PULLEY AS A GUIDE.

CUT THE LOWER FRAME SIDES IN A SIMILAR WAY, USING THE OTHER PULLEY AS THE GUIDE.

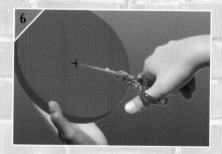

CUT AN X-SHAPED DOUBLE-SLOT IN THE CENTRE OF EACH OF THE PULLEY WHEELS.

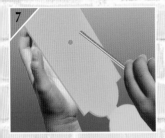

USING A STRAW AS A
GUIDE CUT A ROUND
HOLE IN THE CENTRE OF
EACH HOUSING FLAP.

FILL TWO SHORT LENGTHS OF
STRAW WITH MODELLING CLAY
AND PUSH ONE EACH THROUGH
THE TOP AND BOTTOM
HOUSINGS AND PULLEY WHEELS.

FIX THE HOUSINGS TOGETHER. TIE
ROPE TO A HOLE IN THE BOTTOM
OF THE TOP HOUSING. RUN IT
THROUGH THE LOWER PULLEY AND
BACK THROUGH THE TOP PULLEY.

MAKE A HOLE
AND TIE THE
TOP PULLEY
TO A BEAM.

MORE FOR LESS?

Pulleys work like levers (see page 16). Winding the rope
around two pulleys means that a load can be lifted by
only half the pulling force used
with one pulley. But, as with a
lever, you do not gain this
extra pulling power for
nothing. The load only
moves half as far with two
pulleys, compared to
one. So you pull with
half the force but for
twice
as long.

UPPER PULLEY

PULLEY FRAME

ROPE WINDS
AROUND
BOTH PULLEYS

LOWER
PULLEY

LOAD

FORCE OF
GRAVITY

PULLING
FORCE

HEAVE!
HAUL UP A LOAD
WITH BOTH PULLEYS.
THEN ALTER THE
ROPE TO USE THE
TOP PULLEY ONLY.
DO YOU NEED LESS
OR MORE PULLING
FORCE?

ADD MORE PULLEYS

Each time a pulley is added to the hoist,
the pulling force needed gets smaller. But
the amount of rope becomes longer and
longer, and friction increases too. Try
your hoist with three pulleys.

TOP PULLEY

INTERMEDIATE
PULLEY

BOTTOM PULLEY

TIE A BUCKET TO THE
BOTTOM PULLEY
WITH ROPE.

AROUND ALONG

One of the simplest machines is the screw. It's a slope or ramp wound around a central pole. Like the lever and pulley, the screw alters forces. It can change a small turning or rotating force into a much more powerful force that pulls, splits, lifts, or tightens.

A staircase is a simple slope. A 'spiral' staircase is a slope twisted around a central pole. One big advantage of a 'spiral' staircase is that it takes up less space than a normal one.

PROJECT: MAKE A SCREW LIFT

SCREW LIFT

WHAT YOU NEED

- **large and small card tubes (such as mailing tubes)**
- **clear plastic or cellophane**
- **stiff card**
- **glue**
- **tape**
- **scissors**
- **ruler**
- **compass**
- **polystyrene beads**

1 CUT A LENGTH OF LARGE TUBE, AND A SLIGHTLY LONGER LENGTH OF SMALL TUBE. MEASURE THE CENTRE TO THE EDGE OF BOTH.

2 USE THE MEASUREMENTS TO DRAW TWO CIRCLES ON CLEAR PLASTIC – ADDING 1 CM TO THE OUTER CIRCLE MEASUREMENT.

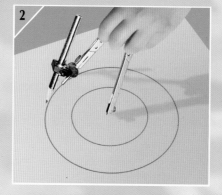

3 MARK TWO FLAPS EITHER SIDE OF A LINE. CUT ALONG THE LINE AND CUT OUT THE CIRCULAR STRIP. MAKE 5 OR 6 OF THESE.

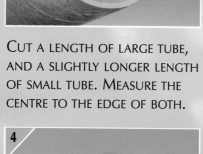

4 MAKE A SLIT AT A SLIGHT ANGLE AT ONE END OF THE NARROWER TUBE. PUSH IN ONE FLAP. PULL THE STRIP DOWN THE TUBE.

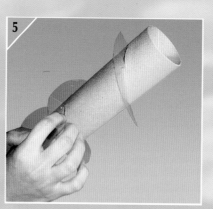

5 MARK THE POSITION OF THE LOWER FLAP, CUT A SLIT AND INSERT IT ALONG WITH THE FIRST FLAP OF A SECOND STRIP.

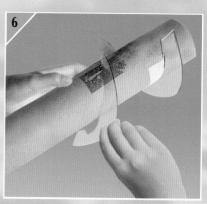

6 PULL THE SECOND STRIP DOWN THE TUBE AND MARK A THIRD SLIT. THE BEGINNINGS OF THE SCREW SHAPE CAN NOW BE SEEN.

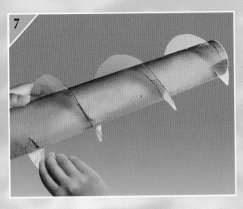

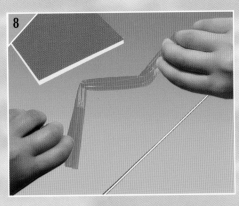

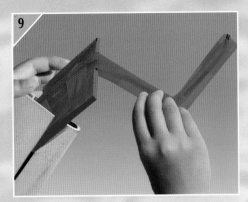

7 REPEAT STEPS 5, AND 6 WITH THE OTHER STRIPS, SO THEY OVERLAP AS A SCREW SHAPE THAT WINDS NEATLY ALONG THE TUBE. TEST-FIT THIS SCREW INTO THE LARGER TUBE SLEEVE. IF IT IS TOO TIGHT, ADJUST THE STRIPS BY MAKING THEIR SLOTS FARTHER APART, SO EACH STRIP ANGLES FLATTER AGAINST THE TUBE. IF THE SCREW IS TOO LOOSE, MAKE THE SLOTS CLOSER.

8 MAKE A HANDLE FROM THREE STRAWS TAPED OR TIED TOGETHER AND BENT IN AN L-SHAPE. GLUE OR TAPE ONE END OF THE L TO A SQUARE OF STIFF CARD. YOU CAN STRENGTHEN THIS HANDLE WITH BENT WIRE IF NECESSARY.

9 INSERT THE SQUARE CARD OF THE HANDLE INTO SLOTS IN ONE END OF THE SCREW. PUT THE SCREW INTO ITS SLEEVE.

TURN TO LIFT

TRY LIFTING SMALL, LIGHT ITEMS LIKE POLYSTYRENE BEAD PACKING. PUT THE LOWER END OF THE SCREW-AND-SLEEVE INTO A BOWL OF THEM, TURN — AND UP THEY COME! CUT A 'WINDOW' IN THE SLEEVE TUBE TO SEE HOW IT WORKS.

TURN OF THE SCREW

The Archimedes' screw uses the same principle as a metal household screw. While the screw stays in position the turning force pulls the material (polystyrene beads) upwards. The Archimedes' screw was invented to lift water from one level to another.

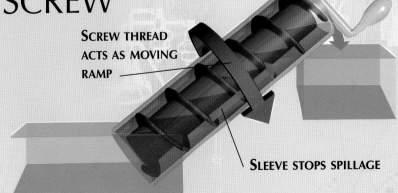

SCREW THREAD ACTS AS MOVING RAMP

SLEEVE STOPS SPILLAGE

GET IN GEAR

Gears can change a force in various ways. Depending on how many cogs or teeth they have, they can increase or decrease the turning speed of a force, and make it more powerful.

Many cogs can be used in different combinations.

Bicycle gears let the rider pedal at the same speed with the same force, whether uphill or down.

Clocks use many cogs to make the hands turn very slowly. The little hand turns just once in 12 hours!

PROJECT: EXPERIMENT WITH COGS

COGS

WHAT YOU NEED

- thick card
- straws
- corrugated card
- cardboard box
- string
- glue
- scissors
- modelling clay

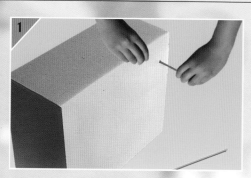

1 MAKE TWO OPPOSING HOLES NEAR ONE END OF A TALL, NARROW BOX. FEED A STRAW THROUGH THE HOLES.

2 CUT OUT A LARGE AND A SMALL DISC FROM STIFF CARD. IN THE CENTRE OF EACH MAKE TWO SLITS IN AN X-SHAPE.

3 CUT STRIPS OF CORRUGATED CARD. GLUE THEM AROUND THE EDGE OF THE DISCS TO MAKE GEAR TEETH.

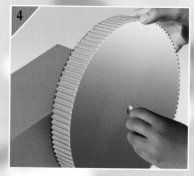

4 PUSH THE LARGER GEARWHEEL FIRMLY ON TO THE STRAW. PUT A LUMP OF MODELLING CLAY ON THE END OF THE STRAW.

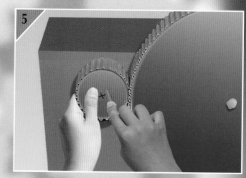

5 HOLD THE LITTLE DISC SO THAT ITS TEETH MESH WITH THE BIG ONE, MARK ITS CENTRE POINT. FIX IT ON AS IN STEP 4. PUT POINTERS ON THE GEARS.

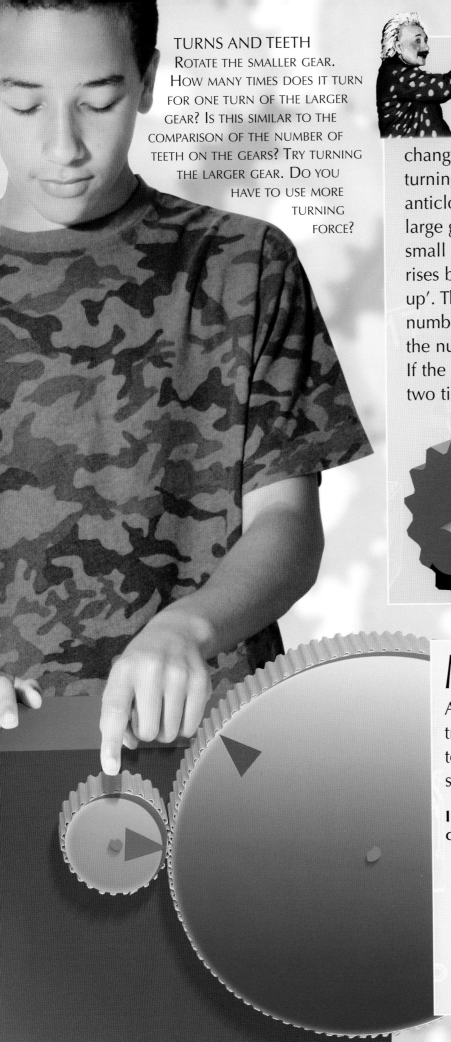

TURNS AND TEETH

ROTATE THE SMALLER GEAR. HOW MANY TIMES DOES IT TURN FOR ONE TURN OF THE LARGER GEAR? IS THIS SIMILAR TO THE COMPARISON OF THE NUMBER OF TEETH ON THE GEARS? TRY TURNING THE LARGER GEAR. DO YOU HAVE TO USE MORE TURNING FORCE?

UP OR DOWN

Two same-sized gears change a clockwise turning force into an anticlockwise one. If a large gearwheel drives a small one, turning speed rises but turning force falls. This is 'gearing up'. The opposite is 'gearing down'. The number of teeth on one gear, compared to the number on the other, is the gearing ratio. If the ratio is 2:1, the turning speed goes up two times but the turning force halves.

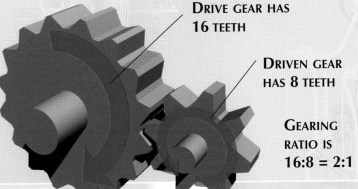

TRANSFER GEARS

DRIVE GEAR HAS 16 TEETH

DRIVEN GEAR HAS 8 TEETH

GEARING RATIO IS 16:8 = 2:1

MORE GEARS

Add more gearwheels to make a gear train. Some machines use gear trains to make different parts turn at their own speeds but keep moving at the same time.

INTERMEDIATE GEARS

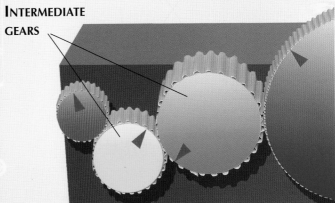

A car's gear shift lever works about a dozen main gearwheels in the gearbox. They mesh in different combinations for first gear, second, third, and so on.

GEARS GALORE

Gears not only change turning speed and force. They can also alter turning direction – at right angles, clockwise to anticlockwise, and so on. There are several main types of gears, each designed to transfer a certain amount of force in a particular way, and also to turn around or run at a certain speed.

PROJECT: MAKE SOME SETS OF GEARS

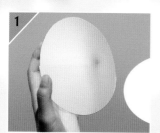

1. CUT TWO CARD DISCS. SLIT TO THE CENTRE, BEND AND GLUE INTO A 45°-ANGLED CONE.

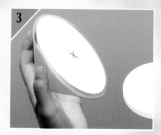

2. CUT TWO MORE CARD DISCS, BIG ENOUGH TO FIT OVER THE ENDS OF THE CONES.

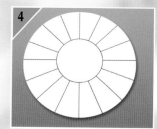

3. MAKE X-SHAPED SLITS IN THE CENTRE OF EACH DISC. GLUE THE DISCS ON TO THE CONES.

4. MARK A CIRCLE ON CARD. DIVIDE IT INTO 16 EQUAL SEGMENTS AND CUT THESE OUT.

WHAT YOU NEED

- cardboard box
- cardboard tube
- stiff card
- thick string
- glue
- large nails
- scissors
- long, thin cardboard box
- straws
- nail
- pencil
- ruler
- compass

5. GLUE 8 SEGMENTS TO EACH CONE WITH GAPS IN BETWEEN.

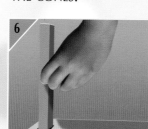

6. GLUE A STRIP OF THICK CARD NEAR THE EDGE OF THE BOX.

7. PUT THE CONES ON STRAW AXLES AND POSITION AS SHOWN.

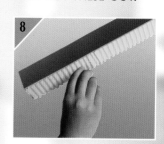

8. STICK A CORRUGATED CARD STRIP TO A LONG, NARROW BOX 'RACK'.

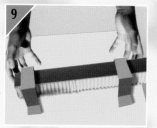

9. CUT CARD BRACKETS TO HOLD THE RACK ON THE BASE BUT LET IT SLIDE.

10. MAKE A GEARWHEEL (SEE PAGE 26) WITH A NAIL AXLE.

11. FIX THE GEARWHEEL'S AXLE TO THE BASE SO IT MESHES WITH THE RACK.

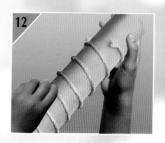

12. WIND THICK STRING AROUND A TUBE AND GLUE IN PLACE.

13

MAKE BRACKETS OF THICK
CARD, WITH HOLES FOR THE
TUBE. FIX THEM TO THE BASE
SO THE TUBE TURNS BUT
CANNOT SLIDE OUT.

14

MAKE ANOTHER GEARWHEEL
AND FIX IT TO THE BASE WITH
A STRAW AXLE, TO MESH WITH
THE TUBE.

WORM AND PINION
THE WORM'S TURNING MOTION MAKES THE PINION
(GEARWHEEL) TURN SLOWLY.

PINION GEAR

WORM GEAR

PINION GEAR

RACK

RACK AND PINION
A TURNING
FORCE AT THE
PINION IS
CHANGED INTO
A SLIDING OR TO-
AND-FRO FORCE AT
THE RACK. OR THE
OPPOSITE CAN HAPPEN.

BEVEL GEARS
WHEN ONE BEVEL GEAR IS TURNED,
THE OTHER ONE ROTATES AT THE SAME
SPEED. THE WAY THAT THE BEVEL GEARS
FIT TOGETHER MEANS THAT THE
DIRECTION OF THE FORCE
CAN BE CHANGED BY 90°.

BEVEL GEARS

NEW DIRECTIONS

The turning force of one bevel gearwheel
transfers through a right angle, 90°, to
the second bevel. The turning force of the worm
transfers to the pinion, through 90°. The force
is now parallel to the axle of the worm.
Unlike the bevel gears, or the rack and
pinion, the worm does not work in reverse:
moving the pinion does not move the worm.

BEVEL GEARS

WORM AND
PINION

RACK AND PINION

FORCES HISTORY

360 BC In Ancient Greece, famous scientist and thinker Aristotle worked out that falling objects gain speed, or accelerate, as they fall. He believed that a heavier object falls faster than a lighter one of the same size and shape.

1581–83 During church services, Galileo Galilei noticed how bell ropes and hanging lamps swing in draughts. He timed the movements using his own pulse (heartbeat). He found the time for each swing was the same, whether the rope swings a long way or a little. He also discovered that all objects with the same size and shape gain speed at the same rate when dropped, no matter what weight they are.

1590 Galileo's *De Motu (On Motion)* described his experiments with falling objects. Around this time, it's said he dropped objects such as cannonballs from the Leaning Tower of Pisa, Italy. He wanted to prove his new ideas about force and motion.

1638 Galileo published one of the greatest science books, *Discourses Concerning Two New Sciences.*

1665–66 Isaac Newton described his three laws of motion. Part of the laws state that force is needed to change the speed or direction of moving objects. Also that every force (action) has an equal and opposite reaction. He also had ideas about gravity as a universal force that acted everywhere.

1676 Robert Hooke described how the stretch of a spring is related to the force pulling it (Hooke's Law).

1684 Newton published his landmark book, *The Mathematical Principles of Natural Philosophy,* usually known as the *Principia.*

1905 Albert Einstein described his theory of special relativity, involving forces and motions at high speeds.

1915 Einstein wrote a scientific report about his theory of general relativity. This replaced Newton's ideas for calculating forces and motions at very fast speeds.

1960 The International General Conference on Weights and Measures defined the unit of force as the newton. One newton accelerates a mass of one kilogram at a rate of one metre per second per second.

GLOSSARY

Accelerate To go faster, gaining more speed for each unit of time. If speed is measured in metres per second, then acceleration is measured in metres per second per second.

Air resistance The force that slows an object passing through air, as the object tries to push aside the tiny particles which make up the air. It is a form of friction.

Decelerate To go slower, losing more speed for each unit of time.

Force A push, pull, squeeze, bend, stretch or similar action that tries to change the movement of an object in some way – its speed, or direction, or both.

Friction A force that opposes movement, when objects rub and scrape past each other. The movement is changed into heat and other forms of energy.

Fulcrum The pivot of a lever, the point at which it tilts or swings.

Gear ratio Usually, a comparison of the number of teeth or cogs on one gearwheel, compared to the number on the other gearwheel.

Gravity A pulling force or attraction that occurs between all objects that have mass, from a single tiny atom to a massive galaxy in space.

Kinetic energy The energy of movement or motion, which depends on the mass of an object and how fast it travels (see also Momentum).

Mass The measurement of the amount of matter in an object, in kilograms.

Momentum The tendency of an object to keep moving in the same direction at the same speed.

Weight The force an object feels due to gravity. Weight depends on the amount of mass an object has, and how strong gravity is. The Moon has less gravity than the Earth and so we would weigh less there than we do here.

INDEX